Katie The Elephant

Written and Illustrated by
Anna Grob

Anna Grob's books are dedicated
to teaching children about animals and nature
http://annagrob.weebly.com

A book by Anna Grob

Copyright © 2018
Katie The Elephant
Forth in the Wild Animal Survival Series

ISBN-13: 9781985783522
ISBN-10: 1985783525

ALL RIGHTS RESERVED

In Loving Memory of my dear father, John Stropkovic. You were the best dad a girl could have. Love you forever dad.

A herd of African elephants celebrated the birth of a new calf in the hot, dry plains of Africa. Darla waited almost two years for her daughter Katie to be born. Darla and the rest of the herd protected Katie from lions and hyenas. She was a bit wobbly at first, but soon was strong enough to stand and walk on her own. Katie followed close to her mother and drank her milk.

"The elephant herd is a loving and protective family," said Darla. Among the herd are aunts, sisters, grandmothers, and cousins. Birtha is the leader of the herd and the oldest female elephant. With her experience and good memory, she leads us to find food and water."

Birtha said, "Every member of our herd is as important to us as the air we breathe, the water we drink, and the food we eat."

Katie's father Tonka, was with a small group of male elephants. He would sometimes spend time on his own. Tonka seemed like a giant to Katie. He was over 13,000 pounds and ten feet tall. Some of the male elephants may get as large as Tonka.

"Come along Katie. We must move on now." said Darla.
Katie's trunk dangled in front of her as she walked beside her mother.
She watched the other elephants use their trunks to pick up leaves and
grass.

"Mama," said Katie. "What is this long floppy thing in front of my
face?"

"It's a long nose called a trunk which you will use for other things as
well," said Darla.

"Why can't I move my trunk like the other elephants do?"

"You must be patient dear. In time, your trunk will get stronger and
you will be able to use it the way we do," said Darla. "An elephant's
trunk is made up of over 40,000 muscles. The tip of the trunk has two
fingers to help grab or pick up grass and twigs. When you are older,
you will carry and move large objects like tree trunks using your own
trunk. We also use our trunks to **communicate** with each other by
touch and sound."

"Cool!" said Katie.

Katie's cousins were excited to play with a new calf. They grabbed and tugged at her trunk to help pull her along.

"Ouch!," cried Katie. "You are hurting me."

Darla stepped in to help her daughter. "Katie is much too young to play rough. You must be gentle with her until she is strong enough to play like the rest of you," she said.

The cousins respected Darla's wishes and gently nudged and asked the new calf to follow them.

Insects buzzed around Katie. She felt the stinging of flies biting her sensitive skin. "Mama help!"

Katie's cousin Dexter came to her aid. "Flap your ears and swat your tail to help shoo away the bugs," he said. "You can use your ears like a fan too to keep you cool."

Dexter laughed as he watched the calf use her ears for the first time. Katie worked hard flapping her ears, but the insects continued to bother her.

"Come, it's time for your mud bath," said Darla. "The mud will help protect your skin from biting insects and sunburn."

As the adult elephants moved toward the waterhole, Katie and her cousins made noise splashing and playing in the water. Her cousins used their trunks to gurgle and splatter themselves with water.

Darla made sure Katie was covered with mud. The mud was very slippery. Katie stumbled and fell as she tried to climb a muddy hill. Darla and the other elephants used their trunks and feet to help lift her. Katie was very tired and took a long nap.

Later that day, Katie noticed two large objects near each side of Darla's trunk. "Mama, what are those two things sticking out of the side of your mouth?" said Katie.

"They are extra long teeth called tusk," said Darla. "Tusk are a very important part of our body and help us survive in the wild. We use our tusk to rip bark off of trees and dig up roots to eat. We also use them to fight off predators.

"Why don't I have any tusk?" asked Katie.

"You will grow two tusk as you get older," said Darla. "Tusks are made of ivory, which **illegal** hunters or **poachers** find valuable to make jewelry, art, and other things. Poachers kill members of the herd to steal the elephant's tusk."

"Can we stop poachers?" asked Katie.

"I hope someday we can," said Darla. "Then elephants and other animals will have a safe place to live forever."

Two years went by. Katie still needed her mother's milk. However, she was able to eat grasses, berries, and other vegetation now. Her trunk was strong enough to carry objects. Katie noticed her tusk's weren't as large as the other young elephants.

"Don't worry dear, your tusk will grow larger in time," said Darla.

As the herd was grazing in the field, Birtha saw poachers sneaking up on the elephants. She stamped her feet, raised her trunk, and stretched out her ears to make herself look larger. Birtha let out a mighty trumpet to warn the poachers, but they did not leave. The calves and young elephants stayed behind the adults as Bertha charged at the intruders.

BANG! "Run, Katie! Run!" shouted Darla. Katie ran as fast as she could and didn't look back. She hid behind thick brush and trees. She could hear the sound of the guns in the distance. Katie was separated from the herd, alone and scared. Then, everything went black.

    Days later, Katie found herself in a strange dark place. The air was cold. Nothing smelled familiar to her. She had been captured by the poachers and sold to Farmer Zack who lived in the United States. Zack knew nothing about raising an elephant. He left a bucket of cows milk in the barn for Katie, but she didn't know how to drink it. She kicked the bucket over with her foot, making a big mess. Zack gave her hay, scraps of fruit, and vegetables he didn't want to sell to the markets. Katie wasn't getting the food she needed, though. She didn't like to feel hungry. She didn't have other elephants to teach her where to find food or water, nor did she have a waterhole or mud to protect her skin from biting insects and sunburn.

Katie rubbed her back against the corner of the fence to help relieve an itch. The force and weight of her body knocked the fence down and she broke free.

Katie was happy to explore in the grass again. She chased the chickens and trampled the corn.

Zack was furious and put chains around her leg to keep her from running free.

Katie was very sad and lonely. She sucked the end of her trunk for comfort like a child would suck their thumb. She truly understood how important an elephant family was. She missed the comfort of her mother wrapping her trunk around her when she was scared. She missed playing and wrestling with her cousins.

One afternoon, Nicole, a volunteer from a nearby zoo, walked her dog Buster down the road. She heard the sound of a trumpet in the distance. At first she thought there was a person learning to play the trumpet. Then she realized, the sound was coming from an elephant. "Why would an elephant be living on a farm?" she said.

Buster barked as they approached the farm. Nicole saw Katie's trunk sticking out of a hole in the side of a barn. She knew in her heart that the young elephant needed to be rescued.

Nicole called her husband Dean who was a zoo veterinarian. Luckily, Dean was able to convince Zack to give up the elephant.

"Gladly," he said bitterly. "She has been nothing but trouble since she came here."

Dean knew Katie needed the proper care and home in order to survive. But where would they put this sweet elephant?

Dean worked closely with zoos to help find a home for Katie. Sadly, many zoos did not have room for an elephant.

Nicole and Dean visited Katie at the farm. Nicole fed her milk from a large bottle while Dean tended to her wounds.

A few days later, they moved Katie to the couple's 30 acre property. There was a pond, open field, and a lot of trees. It had a huge heated and cooled building where Dean kept his collectible cars. It was a good place for Katie to live until they could find her a forever home.

Volunteers brought in truck loads of sand and hay to lie on the floor to keep Katie comfortable. There was still one big problem. Elephants need a pal, and there wasn't another elephant available. Dean had a draft horse named Chester, and of course, Buster the dog. Even though Katie enjoyed their company, she could not speak with them as she would another elephant.

Meanwhile, Nicole and Dean took turns sleeping in the elephant barn to keep Katie company.

Katie was getting stronger from the care and love her new friends gave her. She played with special items which kept her busy, and used her trunk to find treats in holes of a log.

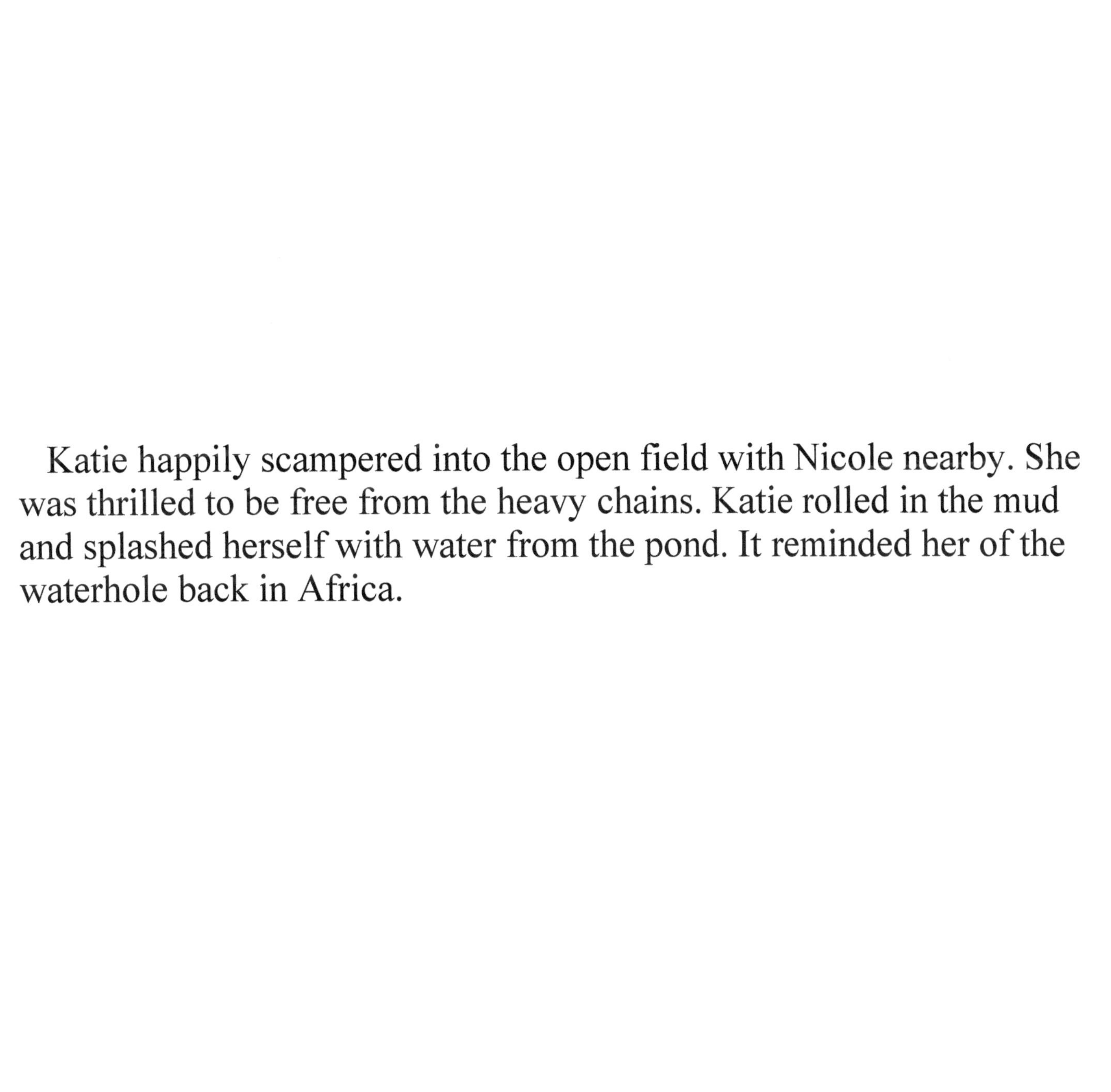

Katie happily scampered into the open field with Nicole nearby. She was thrilled to be free from the heavy chains. Katie rolled in the mud and splashed herself with water from the pond. It reminded her of the waterhole back in Africa.

Finally, Dean found a zoo that decided to use their elephant yard to breed **endangered** Rhinoceros. The zoo had two beautiful elephants, Tulip, and her four year old daughter Daisy. The keepers were sure the elephants would make wonderful companions for Katie.

Katie, Tulip and Daisy, were to be sent to an elephant **sanctuary** in a southern state. Many rescued elephants lived there. It had a big lake and plenty of room for all three of the elephants to live. There were large concrete barriers to keep the elephants safe.

When Katie arrived at the sanctuary, she could smell the other elephants. She was anxious to meet them. She trumpeted loudly and swayed her trunk and body back and forth.

Tulip and Daisy moved closer, sniffing the air with their trunks. They let out a mighty trumpet to say hello to Katie.

After a few days, the elephants were together at last. Daisy ran to greet Katie. They became instant friends. The two elephants wrapped their trunks together in a big hug.

Tulip was a good foster mother to Katie. She welcomed her with a loving touch of her trunk and allowed Katie to drink her milk. Tulip showed Katie where to find food, water, and protected and comforted her when she needed it.

Katie and Daisy played together in the lake. They splashed, gurgled the water and made a lot of noise.

Katie was once again part of a loving elephant herd she could call her family.

Elephants

Elephants are the largest living land mammals in the world. There are two types of elephants: the African and Asian. The African Elephant is larger, and has big ears.

Elephants live in tropical forest, grasslands, woodlands, and the savanna. Elephants are herbivores who eat grass, fruit, plants, herbs, and trees. The bark from the trees contain minerals needed to build and strengthen the elephants' bones.

Teeth- African Elephants have four molars and two tusks. They can have up to six sets of teeth in their lifetime. When a tooth wears down, another one will grow and push the old tooth out in pieces. Tusks are long teeth that can grow several feet in length. Elephant's tusks grow throughout their lives. When elephants use their tusks, they become worn down. Some elephants may have a tusk shorter than the other. Both male and female African elephants have tusks. In Asian elephants, only the males have tusks.

Social - Elephants need other elephants to keep them company and to teach them how to survive. The Matriarch, the oldest female, is the leader and most experienced member of the herd. Can you name who the Matriarch was in this story?

Communication is a way of speaking and connecting with others. Elephants are very smart and have good memories. Like humans, elephants talk to each other. They have many different calls, including loud trumpets, grunts, and rumbles. They also use their trunks, ears, and feet to communicate with other elephants for comfort or to warn predators. Elephants grieve over a lost or deceased member.

A **sanctuary** is a place where rescued animals are cared for and protected.

Endangered animals are those that are in danger of dying out. Elephants and many other animals are endangered. If an animal species dies out, they will become extinct just like the dinosaur. Extinction is forever.

Illegal hunting and poaching is the killing and capturing of animals. It is a very serious problem around the world. Poachers are people who hunt illegally. Poaching can lead to the extinction of elephants and other animals. Many adult elephants are killed for their tusks, leaving calves and young elephants orphaned.

Many animals depend on Elephants to survive. Elephants dig waterholes that help provide water for other animals. They also knock down trees, clearing paths for other species.

To learn more about how you can help elephants, go to my website at
http://annagrob.weebly.com

Wild Animal Survival Series

#1   A Coyote Who Wished He Lived In A Zoo

#2   An African Painted Dog Without A Patch

#3 Gibbon Finds A Friend

#4 Katie The Elephant

Coming Soon
#5 Snow and Amur
Leopards

About The Author

As a life-long animal lover, Anna Grob was led to volunteer as a docent at Brookfield Zoo near Chicago IL. She is privileged to have observed and studied elephants in zoos around the country. With the ever growing ivory trade, and an increase in orphaned elephants, Anna feels it is important to teach readers about the challenges these intelligent animals face in the wild.

Anna Grob is an Award Winning Author/ Illustrator of Children's Books. Her second book, *An African Painted Dog Without A Patch,* won the 2016 National Indie Excellence Book Award under the Children's non-fiction category. Anna's third book, *Gibbon Finds A Friend,* was a finalist for the 2017 Best Book Awards.

Katie The Elephant, is book four in the Wild Animal Survival Series.

Anna can be reached through her website at http://annagrob.weebly.com

Acknowledgments

With much gratitude to my niece Ashley, who supported me through my writing process,
My family and friends
My zoo friends from around the country
My dear husband Donald for his love and patience throughout the years
And a special thanks to David Scholes for the use of his
reference photos of elephants

www.ingramcontent.com/pod-product-compliance
Lightning Source LLC
Chambersburg PA
CBHW040150240726
48664CB00002B/654